Castles Colouring Book

Hand Drawn by APG

Coloured by you

A Key Creations book.

First published 2023.

This edition copyright © Key Creations Ltd 2023.
Illustrations copyright © Key Creations Ltd 2023.

Copyright © Key Creations 2023.

All rights reserved. No part of this publication, or the illustrations within it, may be reproduced, stored in any retrieval system, or distributed in any form or by any means, electronic, mechanical, photocopying, recording, scanning, or otherwise, without prior written permission from the publisher.

Castles Colouring Book

Hand Drawn by APG

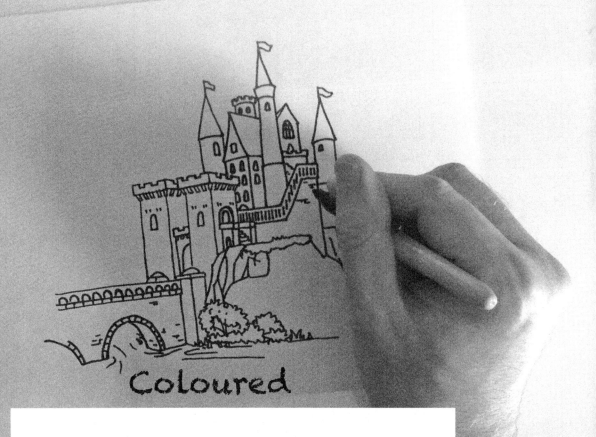

Coloured by _____

Contents pages 7 to 45

Contents pages 47 to 85

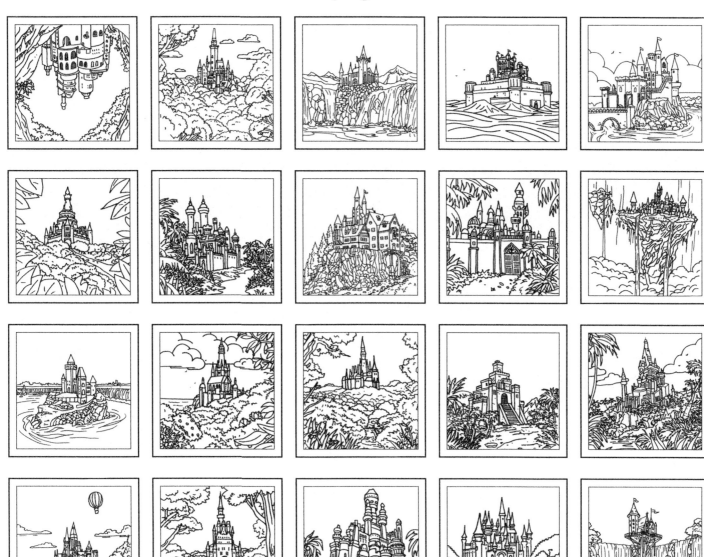

Plus 2 bonus pages

Have a go at colouring some flowers

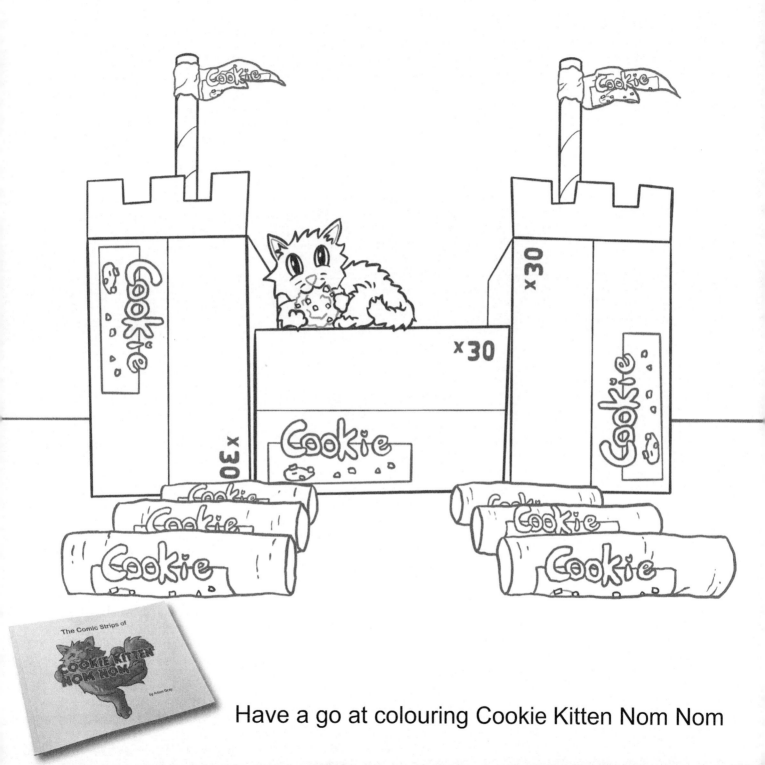

Have a go at colouring Cookie Kitten Nom Nom

Printed in Great Britain
by Amazon